Time Management
secrets

The experts tell all!

About the author
Martin Manser BA (Hons), MPhil
teaches communication skills
at the London College of
Communication. He leads courses
on time management, running
effective meetings, business
writing and leadership. He is the
author of *Presenting*, also in the
business secrets series.

Author's note
Thank you to Hannah and Brian
Murphy for their contributions.

Time Management
secrets

Collins
A division of HarperCollins*Publishers*
77-85 Fulham Palace Road, London W6 8JB

www.BusinessSecrets.net

First published in Great Britain in 2010 by HarperCollins*Publishers*
Published in Canada by HarperCollins*Canada*. www.harpercollins.ca
Published in Australia by HarperCollins*Australia*. www.harpercollins.com.au
Published in India by HarperCollins*PublishersIndia*. www.harpercollins.co.in

1

Copyright © HarperCollins*Publishers* 2010

Martin Manser asserts the moral right to be identified as the author of this work.

A catalogue record for this book is available from the British Library.

ISBN 978-0-00-732446-0

Printed and bound at Clays Ltd, St Ives plc

Contents

Learn how to use your time effectively

There was a saying in our home as I grew up: "Even a world leader only has 24 hours in a day!" We all want to make sure we live well, that we make the best use of our time, but it is limited for each one of us. How can we make the best of our time?

We all have different personalities and have various demands made on our time. Some of us are very organized, others less so.

Over my working life, I've learnt a number of techniques to help make good use of time. There are two basic ideas: one is to work efficiently – to see that I have systems in place so that things go smoothly, making the best use of the resources available to me. But I have learnt to do more than that; I also want to live and work effectively – to make something of my life, to make it count, to achieve something definite, good and right.

Over the 30 years of my working life, I have had to ask myself some hard questions: what do I want out of life? What do I want to achieve? What kind of person am I? How can I develop as a person? How do I want to spend my time? How should I value my time?

So this book is more than being simply about how we spend our time. It's about how we spend our life. Here are 50 **secrets** I've learnt, divided into seven chapters:

■ **Know yourself.** If you know what kind of person you are and what you want to get out of life, you can begin to set priorities.

■ **Know your work.** Our business life is a major part of our lives. Knowing the underlying purposes of your job will help focus your attention on seeing how well you use your time.

■ **Get organized.** Here are tips on working effectively, e.g. by keeping a diary, setting up systems and drawing up schedules.

■ **Work better.** It is important to use your time proactively, setting priorities and working well at tasks, however small they are.

■ **Work better as a team.** We don't work individually, in isolation from one another, so it's vital to develop good working relationships within a team with successful delegation and well-run meetings.

■ **Communicate more effectively.** How do we stop all our time being taken up by email, computers and the Internet? Face-to-face and phone communication are also vital in good time management, as are good listening, reading and writing skills.

■ **Take control of your time.** Effective use of time takes place as you learn to manage time well by remaining focused on tasks, minimizing interruptions and using slack time that may come unexpectedly.

If you follow these seven **secrets** you will know how to spend your time well, how to live effectively, how to make the most of the adventure of life. I wish you all the best!

You can learn to take control of how you spend your time.

Know yourself

This opening chapter will help you understand the broader issues concerning how you spend your time. Defining what you want out of life, what goals you have and when and how you work best will help you understand your overall priorities. This will then translate into the way in which you go about managing your time.

1.1

Start with some dreams

Before you start looking at how you spend your time at work, it is very useful to think about your life more widely. Do you have a clear vision for your life? What are you most passionate about? Answering these questions will help you decide on what really matters in life and so how you choose to spend your time.

Here are five 'Ds' to think about:

1 **Drive.** Think about what really fires you up. What motivates you? What is it that gives you energy and a great sense of personal fulfilment? What values in life do you hold? What do you care deeply about?

2 **Dream.** What have you always wanted to do? Where do you see yourself in a year's time? What about in five years' time? Dream some dreams!

"Focusing your life solely on making a buck shows a poverty of ambition. It asks too little of yourself. And it will leave you unfulfilled" **Barack Obama, US President**

3 **Develop.** What natural skills, abilities or talents do you have that you could develop further?

4 **Discuss.** Chat through the answers to some of these questions with friends. Are you being honest or completely unrealistic about yourself. Are there seeds of some possibilities that could become real?

5 **Define.** It will help you greatly if you can set clear and positive goals: "I'd like to…", "In five years' time I want to be able to…" You can then break down these goals into more immediate aims, such as steps to obtain a qualification, gain experience or learn new skills. Think about what the next steps would be in order to fulfil the goals and aims that you have set for yourself.

Focus on what motivates you, the things you would like to achieve and what personal fulfilment means to you.

1.2

Think about your personal goals

Goals can be related to your work, to your family life or to life in your community. They might even relate to playing a role on the world stage. Whatever the case, it is only once you have set yourself a goal that you can plan how to translate it into reality.

Your goal might be, for example, "to become a partner in this firm by the age of 30", or "to spend 50% more time with my family" or "to help underprivileged children". Whatever the goal, once you have settled on your main objectives, you can begin to break them down into smaller steps to enable them to be realized.

case study Five years ago, Alex knew he wanted to work in Thailand: that was his dream and passion. He was already qualified as a teacher in his home country, but he needed further training to refine his skills and learn the local language. He couldn't give up his full-time job, so he decided to spend an

A useful exercise at this stage is to prepare a pattern diagram of the various activities surrounding your goal. This is a diagram you creatively draw that captures what you perceive to be the main aspects of your central idea. To do this, you should:

■ Take a blank sheet of A4 paper, arranging it in landscape format.
■ Write your central goal (a word or a few words, not a whole sentence) in the middle of the paper.
■ Write around that central word other key words that relate to it.
■ Keep branching out various other aspects of the goal that come into your mind.
■ If you get stuck at any point, answer the fundamental questions: who?, why?, where?, what?, when? and how? Doing this will stimulate your thinking process.
■ At this stage, do not reject any thoughts.
■ You can colour different key words to show which relate to each other.
■ You can number the different key words, too, in order of importance.

Hopefully you'll find it a useful way to think about your goals, what other aspects of your life they may affect, and get a clearer picture of what steps you'll need to take to achieve them.

Define your goals and think creatively about the different aspects of them.

evening every week for two years learning the local language from a friend, and studying the background and culture of the country. His focused, practical steps taken towards this long-term goal eventually paid off, and Alex is now teaching in Thailand with a real sense of fulfilment.

1.3

Know when you work best

Each one of us has a period of time during the day when we work best. It could be early morning, mid-morning after coffee, after lunch or in the evening. You should be doing the most important or difficult work when you are most alert.

When working out which time of day you work best, remember that eating a heavy meal can make your work rate slower, and so you are more likely to make mistakes. You should guard your most productive time and not use it doing non-productive tasks. The saying goes, "time spent sharpening a pencil is never wasted", but you shouldn't use your high-energy time to sharpen pencils!

case study Stan works in an office and knows that he works best in the morning. Every day as far as possible he completes the parts of his work that need more concentrated thought between 9am and 1pm. In the afternoon, he makes himself

■ **Morning people.** For many people, the best time of day is the morning, when they are most alert, have the highest energy levels and so do their best work. There are two well-known proverbs for morning people: "An hour in the morning is worth two in the evening." "Lose an hour in the morning and you'll be all day hunting for it."

■ **Energy through the week.** The same principle also applies to days of the week. If you work best on Mondays and Tuesdays, schedule routine meetings for later in the week.

For example, standing around in a queue at 8am waiting to hand in your car at a garage is frustrating for you if your highest energy level is at that time. If you can hand it in later in the day, once your hardest work has been done, then that will be better for you. Keeping as far as possible to this time will help you avoid becoming distracted by all the constant interruptions that can turn you away from fulfilling the task you have to complete.

You shouldn't be using your most productive time on routine tasks.

available for meetings or routine admin tasks. He has to be flexible to some extent, but he gets more work done by grouping tasks into those that need concentration and those that are purely adminis- trative than by shifting from one to the other.

1.4

Track how you spend your time

An important step in managing your time is to know how you are actually spending your time. A very useful exercise to work this out exactly is to record the minutiae of your day.

There are two ways of working out how long you spend on different tasks: one is to estimate, the other is to record accurately. The second way is better. If you do this for a day (or ideally, longer), you will probably be surprised that many tasks take longer than you think.

Set up a chart on hard copy or on a spreadsheet broken down into the following columns:

Description	Start time	End time	Time in minutes	Priority

For the priority column, choose a level of priority from 1 to 5, with 1 being the greatest priority, 5 the least.

one minute wonder Calculate the hourly rate that you are costing your organization:

■ Take the productive part of each day, which is probably somewhere between 50% and 80% – let's say 65%.
■ Say you work 8 hours per day x 65% = 5.2 hours per day that are productive. Say you earn £30,000 per year; then double that to count in benefits and employment overheads = £60k per year.
■ Divide that by 52 weeks minus 6 weeks for holidays/illnesses = 46 weeks x 5 days x 5.2 hours per day = 1196 hours per year.
■ Round to 1200 hours and divide £60k by 1200 hours = £50 per hour.
■ This means that you cost your company or organization £50 for every productive hour you work – an incentive not to waste time!

Recording this level of detail will almost certainly reveal things that you were not aware of about your working day. It may, for example, demonstrate that you spend more time than you had throught in travelling or doing routine tasks (one of my colleagues calculated that he spends a total of 15 minutes every day walking from his computer to the printer and back), or that you spend less time than you should in planning and thinking.

When working out the priority column, consider the following:

■ Which tasks are central to your role.
■ Which tasks could be delegated.
■ Which tasks could be done more effectively.
■ Which tasks you should not be doing in the first place.

Calculate your time on different tasks and your hourly rate with overheads.

1.5

Get on top of stress

If we had no stress in our lives, maybe nothing would get done. But most of us have too much stress – enough to make us read a book about time management! We find ourselves unable to make decisions and we lose a sense of proportion about life as we become more and more burdened.

We become frustrated at how little progress is being made on the project we've been working hard at, despite all our efforts. We think we're too busy even to take a holiday. If such feelings are familiar to you, it is vital that you find ways that work for you to manage and reduce the stress in your life. Here are some guidelines (see also 4.8):

case study In Ron's first eight years of working independently, he put in extremely long hours. He was often so exhausted that he couldn't relax even when away from work, and his relationship with his wife and children suffered. His stress built up and took an emotional and physical toll. He eventually realized that he needed to learn how to build a

■ **Schedule in regular times of rest.** If you know you've got a very busy week, try to make the weekend or the next week less busy.

■ **Learn to say no.** Don't try to control everything in the universe: set yourself realistic goals (see also 5.5).

■ **Plan holidays in advance.** A colleague plans a weekend away every six weeks, to have something to look forward to.

■ **Allow time to be with your partner and family.** Schedule family time into the diary if need be!

■ **Take up a new hobby.** Or volunteer to help a local charity. Working with others will take you out of yourself.

■ **Spend time with friends.** Old friends and new friends.

■ **Develop a sense of humour.** It's one of the best antidotes for stress.

■ **Engage in physical exercise.** For example, jogging, cycling, swimming, walking or dancing.

■ **Absorb yourself with the arts or music.** Make time to go to an art gallery, the theatre or a concert.

■ **Attend to your spiritual side.** Spend time in a form of prayer or meditation to help connect you with more than the physical world.

Think of practical ways to reduce the stress in your life.

more balanced lifestyle. So Ron scheduled in more family time. He also developed regular habits of walking around the block (5, 10, 20, 40 minutes depending on the time available) and developed a support group of friends who met regularly. He became more resilient and had 'coping mechanisms' in place to help him in times of stress.

1.6

Prepare to change

An important part of this book is to help you identify what you need to change in order to manage time more effectively. But do you lack the motivation to change? Here are eight ideas to help you become more familiar with the idea of change in your life.

1 **Try new ways of doing things.** Move beyond the "I've always done it this way" mentality. You can begin with something relatively small, like driving a different way to work. Set realistic goals to make a small noticeable adjustment. Don't get off at the closest bus stop to your work, for example, but the stop before and walk the rest of the way. If you can do that a couple of times a week, it's a start.

2 **Admit you don't know everything.** I have been helped by the saying, "It's a strong person who admits their weaknesses". This means you will listen more, acknowledge errors and be willing to receive feedback and learn from mistakes.

3 **Ask more questions.** Remember your underlying aims and goals, and think creatively about new ways to reach them.

"When we are no longer able to change a situation, we are challenged to change ourselves"

Victor Frankl, Austrian psychiatrist and Holocaust survivor

4 **Move on from past experiences.** Learn from your past, but don't worry about specific events unduly.

5 **Don't be afraid of failure.** The American inventor Thomas Edison said, "I have not failed. I've just found 10,000 ways that won't work."

6 **Build in regular reviews.** These could be in advance of your regular appraisal.

7 **Evaluate your goals.** An aspect of setting goals is so that you can see if you are reaching them or not.

8 **Use friends to help you change.** Gather friends around you with whom you can share your goals and frustrations. Allow them to help you and guide you where necessary.

Mentally prepare yourself for new ways of doing things.

Know your work

Alongside knowing what kind of a person you are, it is important to think specifically about your job. You need to be clear about your role and the responsibilities that you are expected to fulfil. We all need help at times to maintain concentration on all aspects of our work: to stop putting off doing routine or difficult tasks, to overcome poor motivation, to keep focused and make good decisions. This chapter has techniques to help you do that.

2.1

Clarify your job

We all spend a lot of time being busy, but it is important to stop and be clear about what our job is all about. We can then think how effective we are at actually carrying out our job.

1 Write down what you think is the general purpose of your job. For example, to lead a team in providing excellent customer service over the telephone.

2 Now write down the main areas that together make up the general purpose of your job. For example: leadership; monitoring statistics; providing customer service; training and developing staff; time management; and monitoring staff performance by holding appraisals and one-to-one meetings.

3 Now write down the activities that you need to do to actually fulfil the work in the main areas you listed in the previous point. For example, training and developing staff: maintaining a training rota and booking time out for the team to do individual training and booking staff on any compulsory training.

4 Now think about how you actually spend your time. Using what you have written in the first three points, how much of your time is spent fulfilling the general purpose, the main areas you listed and the actual activities? What would you like to do less of? What would you like to do more of? Hopefully, you are spending most of your time in this way, rather than in general administration, for example (unless this is your job).

5 If you work as part of a team, be clear about how your job, areas and activities fit in with those of your colleagues, your boss and any subordinate people working for you.

6 Review the first four points regularly with your boss and at your appraisals. Such meetings can be useful occasions for you to consider, for example, what is preventing you from fulfilling your main purpose and discover where you are getting sidetracked into other areas or activities.

Make sure that you actually spend most of your time on the main part of your job.

2.2

Stop putting things off

You may be the kind of person who constantly puts off doing tasks that are boring or difficult. The longer you delay getting round to the tasks, the greater will be your resistance to them and, therefore, the harder it will be to actually complete them.

You may avoid doing a task for various reasons: the job is boring or routine; the task is too difficult; the work has no deadline; the goals are unclear; or you simply have so many things to do that you don't know where to start. Or you may be afraid of failure or rejection if you perform badly.

In certain circumstances, it is right to make a decision not to undertake a task: when you need to collect all the information or when you need time to think. But, on many other occasions, it simply boils down to delaying doing something.

Here are some ways to help you break through the barrier of extended procrastination:

"You may delay, but time will not, and lost time is never found again"

Benjamin Franklin, 18th-century American statesman and polymath

1 Break a large task down into more manageable sections (see Secret 4.5). Tackle one part, not necessarily the first part. The fact that you have completed a small section will then make you feel better about the whole.

2 Start on the hardest part. Do this in your most productive, high-energy time (see 1.3).

3 Give yourself a reward, but only after you have actually completed a task.

4 Work on routine tasks in your least productive time or as a break from periods of concentrated activity.

Procrastination ultimately makes a job more difficult.

2.3

Keep your concentration

We've all known times when our energy levels have decreased and we've lost motivation to complete a task. You need to set yourself realistic targets that use your skills and help you work well. Use rewards, if you like, to emphasize a sense of achievement.

■ **Set yourself a goal.** "By coffee break, I want to have achieved…". The goal should be challenging and should stretch you slightly, but it shouldn't be too demanding or unrealistic. Plan to have a break after you have met your target and completed the task; resist the urge to take sudden unplanned breaks.

case study My aim in writing this book was to complete four units each day. In this unit, for example, I wrote rough notes for the area I wanted to cover and then wrote this case study – I found it's easier to work from a specific example back to general principles – and finally the main text and intro. I tried not to interrupt myself by checking

■ Target a task. Ideally, your target should be to complete a task rather than simply fill a length of time, so say to yourself, "I want to have all the sales figures collated by three o'clock," rather than "I'm going to spend an hour on the sales figures and see how far I get".

■ Give it a time period. It is helpful to aim for a task that'll take 30-90 minutes. Anything shorter is too short to stretch you and above that could be unrealistic. If you complete the task quicker than the time you have allowed, then good. If you haven't, don't despair. Don't give up or stop if the end is in sight. If you stop, you will lose the momentum you have built up and it will take you some time to regain it. Continue to work steadily until you have completely finished the task.

■ Interruptions and set-backs. If you have to stop or are interrupted, note briefly – write or type a key word – where you are up to in your work, so that you can pick it up again easily. If you meet an insurmountable difficulty that stops your progress, set a smaller target and think creatively about a different approach to the difficulty. Or tackle a different part of the task and return to the troublesome part later.

Set a target to complete a task rather than simply fill a period of time.

emails and, after finishing, read through the unit and looked at its place in the sequence. Writing took different amounts of time, depending on the subject of the unit, but I found setting a specific target helpful. I gave myself a break after writing two units and then after the day's final two. The target was challenging, but realistic and achievable.

2.4

Overcome low motivation

Try to become aware of why you have low motivation at times. Learn to challenge the thoughts that prevent or stop you from moving on and actually completing a task.

Here are some common thoughts about poor motivation, and suggestions on how to deal with them:

■ **"I don't feel like doing it."** Do what you know is right, regardless of your feelings. The day I left my office to discuss what turned out to be my first book, I ignored the internal thoughts buzzing around in my mind of "why are you bothering to go to this meeting?" It was good that I did go, as that book later sold many thousands of copies.

case study Marcus found himself sitting next to the CEO of his organization on a plane. Rather than panicking at the thought of talking to someone so high up in the company, he challenged the thoughts of failure and fear that he might say the wrong thing. He outlined, gently but clearly, what he saw as

■ **"I don't know where to begin."** Cut up the task into smaller, more manageable units.

■ **"I don't feel like working."** Set yourself simple tasks to complete. Imagine it's a task you enjoy. Be firm with yourself, but then give yourself a reward when you have completed the task.

■ **"It's boring."** Set yourself a time limit to complete part of the task in, say, ten minutes.

■ **"I work better just before a deadline."** Okay, that may be the case, but you can still plan your time better.

■ **"I'm afraid I'll fail."** Remember that the person who never made mistakes never made anything. Don't panic; think what is the worst that could happen? Learn from your past mistakes. Be courageous. If necessary, learn new skills.

■ **"I've always done it this way."** Take a risk. Do something differently. Think outside the box. Change your perspective. Innovation is an opportunity to grasp, not a threat. Grasp the opportunity.

Do what you know is right, regardless of your feelings of apathy.

the organization's strengths and weaknesses and how he saw the company's future. The result was that, a few days later, he got a phone call which led ultimately to his promotion. By being firm with himself, Marcus kept his nerve and didn't panic. He took a risk and spoke up, which paid off.

2.5

Sharpen up your decision-making

We all make decisions constantly in life – which clothes to wear each day, what food we eat and so on – but it can be difficult making decisions about things that have greater significance.

Here are some guidelines on coming to a decision. It can be helpful to write down all the choices you face. If there are a large number, reduce the choices to the most important. Ask yourself the following questions (I find it helpful to write down the answers):

■ What are the advantages and disadvantages of each option?
You may need to put greater significance on some advantages and disadvantages to discern the way forward.

case study I was due to go on an intensive course in London for a month. I had to make a decision about where to stay during the course: at home, incurring four hours of travel each day; with my brother in central London; or with my uncle in the suburbs? I listed the various options, weighing up financial

■ **What are the effects of choosing each option?** For example, choosing a new job that would mean working a long way from home for weeks on end would have a significant effect on your family life.

■ **What would happen if you made no decision at all?** How would that relate to your fulfilling your long-term goals?

■ **What is the time scale for making a decision?** For example, do you have a meeting coming up at which you need to report your decision? If so, allow time to write your report. If you have no particular time frame, then give yourself one to spur yourself on.

■ **Who can I seek advice from on this matter?** Ideally, you'll seek advice from someone with greater experience than yourself, but any good friend can work as a 'sounding board'.

■ **Think 'outside the box'.** Be creative and imaginative in thinking up further possible solutions. It might be helpful to take a break from the fine detail of trying to come to a decision in order to help you focus on the bigger picture at this point.

■ **Don't ignore your instincts.** What is your instinctive response to the different choices that you face?

Be logical in your approach to decision-making, but consider what your instincts are telling you too.

cost, travelling time, and access to computer facilities. Through analysis, I realized that the most important factor wasn't cost or travelling time, but how effectively I could continue working. This informed my decision to stay with my brother, using my laptop and his printer and modem.

2.6

Be flexible about where you work

If you can work from home at least some of the time, you will probably get a lot more work done. You will be able to be flexible and control your own schedule with no one constantly checking up on you.

Learn to make good use of your time wherever you are. If you travel regularly by train or plane, for example, plan to take work with you that you can easily do while on the move. If you can work from home on certain days, you will find that you can clear paperwork efficiently or else have time to think creatively, away from disractions. If you work from home regularly, you will need to:

case study Jo has worked from home for nearly 30 years. It has had many advantages, including having to attend far fewer meetings, minimal travelling time – a commute of 30 seconds – and being at home when her children came home from school. She has missed regular contact with business colleagues,

■ Be disciplined. Set regular times to start and finish work each day. Schedule breaks into your timetable.

■ Set up your own support system. At work, you have the office chat with your colleagues. At home, it is just you. You need to take the initiative in setting up times to meet with friends.

■ Avoid distractions. Tell friends and family that you are at work and should not be disturbed. Some will listen; some won't, but you need to set definite boundaries.

■ Set up your own office space. Preferably, this should be in a separate room, to maintain a boundary between work and home.

■ Arrange professional help. You'll need, for example, insurance if clients visit your premises or if you have specialist equipment. I have been greatly helped over the years by a friend who is a retired bank manager. He has helped me check costings, plan cash flows and so on.

Working from home occasionally will probably mean you get a lot more work done.

however, and has had learn to be involved in lunchtime activities by going to the gym or making appointments to meet friends on a regular basis. This has helped lessen a sense of isolation felt by many who work from home, and maintained her all-round health and well-being.

Get
organized

Clearing your desk of unnecessary clutter will help you think and work better. Keeping a diary and compiling a 'to do' list will keep you on top of things. If something's written down, you don't need to keep it constantly at the front of your mind, which you can then use for more creative tasks. Set up systems to help you with routine tasks, and draw up detailed schedules for projects. Then, if you find you're running late, you can take action to get back on track.

3.1

Clear your desk

Part of being organized is to have all that you need near you, not being surrounded by untidy piles of papers and things that you don't need. Your aim is to organize things so that you can work efficiently and can retrieve things you need quickly when you want them. Arrange the equipment you use regularly so that it is close by in a way that works best for you.

Here are five practical steps you can take to organize a better workspace for yourself:

1 Clear away from your desk things that are not related to your current project. This will help you focus your attention on what really matters at work. Put things that you need constantly within easy reach, so that you don't have to keep on getting up from your chair.

2 If you have an in-tray and an out-tray, use them. Occasionally, start at the bottom of the in-tray and throw away or file papers that you are storing there.

one minute wonder At the end of each day have a quick tidy of your desk. Keep all but the most essential stationery out of sight in drawers or cupboards and have only work relating to current projects at hand – everything else should be filed.

3 Spend time tidying up your work environment – pens, papers, mugs, glasses, pencils, paper clips and so on. Put away things that you don't use very often.

4 Archive very old material. Label old papers or boxes clearly with their contents and dates.

5 Make sure your computer equipment is arranged so that you can work efficiently, safely and comfortably. Your computer screen should be at the right height – it is generally recommended that the monitor should be at least 63 cm (25 inches) away from your eyes and the top of the monitor screen is just below eye level. Make sure that you are sitting in a well-designed chair that is adjusted to the right height. In the area under your desk, install a foot rest. Clear away the area under your desk so that there is enough room to allow you to stretch your legs.

Clear your desk of things you don't need constantly, so you can think clearly and concentrate better.

3.2

Keep a diary

Keeping a diary means that you can keep on track of things. A diary can also be useful for setting reminders of times when you need to chase colleagues for reports and responses. Remember that, if you use an Outlook diary in an office environment, many people can see your appointments or the time you have blocked off.

■ Paper or electronic? It doesn't matter if you use a paper diary or an electronic one, what is important is that you have one – and only one, for all your business and personal appointments. In it, you can also note actions/tasks to do, people to see, emails or phone calls to make etc. For a few years I had two diaries, one for work and one for the rest of my life, but I found that became unworkable.

> **case study** Mike finds he works best with an A4 week-to-view diary, with space for Saturdays and Sundays. In the space for Friday, he has blocked out a separate area for forward planning: items that will go forward to the next week. At the end of every

■ Schedule sensibly. Spend some time thinking through the scheduling of appointments: what would happen if a meeting runs late? Do you want a meeting over lunch? Remember when you work most productively and protect that time for what is important.

■ Give sufficient details. In your diary entry, write enough details for you to be able to understand what's meant when you read it at a later date. You may also want it to be clear enough for someone else to read it too. Enter the location of a meeting, for example, if it is not in your office, along with the time and person or people you are meeting.

■ Pencil or pen? If the diary is hard copy, some people prefer to use a pencil so that changes can easily be made.

■ Set reminders. Use electronic reminders to set recurring items, such as booking a car for a service, paying bills, sending birthday cards. Set reminders a sufficient time in advance of the deadline to give you time to think and work through any practical actions.

■ Use a wall planner. This can help you see the bigger picture. On it, mark holidays and specific moments or periods in a project.

■ What about other info? You can put information such as phone numbers, email addresses and contact information in your diary but, if you use a hard copy and change it annually, you might find it better to use a separate address book for this.

Keeping a diary helps you take control of how you are to spend your time.

working day, Mike plans the following day's work, appointments, phone calls, etc. On a Friday, he works through the forward planning to plan the following week's work. Using this method, he has learnt to take basic control of his working day.

3.3

Set up systems

There are probably many tasks that you do as part of your job that you do every day, week or month. If you work on organizing these as efficiently as possible, you will free up a bit more time and be able to work more effectively.

Identify tasks that you perform regularly and that form part of your work. Some items, such as checking emails, are so regular that you do not need to list them – they are your constant 'lifeblood'.

What I am thinking of here are such things as:

■ **Daily and weekly tasks.** Filling in timesheets, making follow-up calls to new contacts, scanning periodicals for relevant information.

case study Depak works in a food-processing factory. He has to prepare monthly accounts for his boss. They are always due on the Monday of week 4 in the following month. As soon as the bank statement arrives, Depak begins his work, analysing

■ **Monthly tasks.** These could include writing progress reports, producing monthly newsletters and updating your website. Training might fall into this group too, as well as pursuing new leads or contacts and making preparations for exhibitions and business conferences.

■ **Yearly tasks.** These tasks might include carrying out annual staff assessments and preparing year-end accounts.

■ **Identify tasks for the diary.** Put the large tasks in your diary as recurring items.

■ **Look at more detail.** Break down the tasks into smaller, more manageable, units where necessary, and list the people you need to contact in each case, either by seniority or in order of the different stages of the task.

■ **Now make checklists.** Compile checklists for the tasks you regularly undertake so that you can tick them off as you complete them. Develop checklists for as many of these tasks as you can, so that every time the same task comes up you do not have to rethink the different stages, the various people you need to contact and so on.

Schedule your regular tasks and develop systems for completing them.

invoices, bills and vouchers throughout week one. He spends week 2 reconciling the figures and week 3 finalizing details and addressing any queries, so that, by week 4, Depak is ready to make a full summary presentation to his boss.

3.4

File it

Filing papers means that you can access information easily when you need it. You do not need to keep all the information on your desk. A good filing system follows certain principles, and these apply equally for hard copies and digital files. Here are some important guidelines to follow in filing.

■ **Use a system.** Follow a system that works for you and that you will remember. Alphabetically usually works well for most aspects of work. An alternative is by date order.

■ **Be clear.** Give your file a name. If you are working electronically and want to give a name that includes a date, be sure always to use the same date format: for example 100307 for 7 March 2010.

■ **Be specific.** For large projects, split it into aspects, with a file for each.

> **case study** A publisher recently contacted me about reusing material from a book I worked on 15 years ago. I knew I had the text but the question was: would my archive and filing systems enable me to retrieve the required information easily? The text was in two halves: I quickly found the first part, but

■ Be helpful to yourself. I sometimes write key contact details, such as a phone number or email address, on the front of a file.

■ Think into the future. Write notes to yourself. You may think that you will remember a particular point, but will you in a week, a month or a year? Write yourself a note, date it and pop it in the file.

■ Keep it orderly. Within a hard-copy file, keep material that is most recent on top. Every few weeks, I sort through a file and put pages that I have dealt with behind a coloured sheet of paper, on which I write, "Behind all dealt with".

■ Be a step ahead. If you are working electronically, set up 'Temp' or 'Spare' file directories for you to use when the occasion arises.

■ File regularly. Spend time regularly filing your papers. Use a time of day when you are least productive to do this.

■ Clear as you go. Don't file everything. Sometimes the best place to file a piece of paper is the waste-paper basket!

If you decide on an electronic filing system, think about what method of filing works for you. You may not want to spend huge amounts of time filing emails into folders, one for each project. You could have one large inbox archive and one large outbox archive: filing your emails in this way may be a better use of your time.

Develop filing systems that work for you, and get into the habit of using them.

had to check through archived electronic material for the second half. As everything was clearly labelled, I was able to search through and find the appropriate material in about 20 minutes. I was grateful that, from the outset of my working life, I had developed a clear system for storing data.

3.5

Create an action list

When you have broken down your goals into smaller, manageable tasks, you can set about preparing an action list for the tasks you need to tackle and finish for a particular day. A daily action plan is where all your tasks come together.

You can list tasks from long-term goals, tasks on particular projects you are working on now and regular meetings. It is important that you don't focus just on what's imminent and urgent but that you also look beyond, to tasks that actually fulfil your long-term goals.

When I write up an action list, or 'to do' list for the day, I include everything I need to get done, so I don't have to rely on my memory. I list the major tasks on current projects that I must complete that day, meetings, and colleagues and friends I need to email. It is important to be realistic, however, and not to try to stretch oneself excessively.

case study Today's action plan for me included working on four units of this book, discussing a contract, a lunchtime appointment with friends, a regular afternoon update meeting, asking a colleague to do some research, arranging meetings

one minute wonder Look at your action plan regularly during the day. I didn't used to do this, but simply listed tasks – then wondered why I didn't complete them! So glance at the list ever now and then to keep yourself on track.

Some people note by the side of each task an estimate of the time they think it will take. I don't do this – the time to do this might take me too long! I prefer simply to list the items in various places on one blank A4 sheet (arranged in landscape format):

■ **Left-hand side.** Major tasks to be completed today (this usually consists of only one or two items).
■ **Centre top.** People I need to contact by telephone (t) or email (e) at my mid-morning coffee break.
■ **Right-hand side.** Routine tasks to be completed at odd moments during the day, such as while waiting for someone on the phone, while waiting for the computer to perform a task, or to be tackled during less productive parts of the day.

I try to schedule in thinking time as a separate item – how to approach a colleague about a difficult issue, for example. It is also important to allow time for travel and, as far as possible, interruptions.

A daily action plan is essential.

and emailing birthday wishes to a friend in Africa. As I completed each task, I crossed it out. If for some reason a task was not completed, I put a circle round that item and carried it forward to be included in the next day's action list.

3.6

Set a realistic schedule

A schedule is not only a basis on which you plan individual tasks that are part of a project, it is also essential to help you keep track of where you are up to when the project is underway.

Here are some guidelines to help you plan a schedule:

1 Break down your project into smaller units or tasks. This is always helpful so you can keep a good track of the work flow and your use of time.

2 Order the different tasks: some need to be completed sequentially, so you'll need to get certain tasks done before you can go on to embark on others.

one minute wonder Think about a task or project you are currently working on. Do you have a schedule in place? If so does it take into account the points outlined here? When you finish the job, look back to see how accurate your scheduling was.

"The last 10% of the project takes the last 90% of the time" Anonymous

3 Work out how long each task will actually take in terms of hours or days. Be as precise as possible.

4 Work out the resources and logistics. What will you need to complete the project in terms of money and staffing?

5 Enter on a chart the start and finish dates for the whole project and for each particular task. You can also enter on the chart the earliest possible start and finish dates and the latest possible start and finish dates so that you can see what flexibility you have. The kind of chart on which you enter these details is called a **Gantt chart** – one that illustrates the duration of certain tasks in a project alongside units of time, such as weeks or months.

6 Remember that some of the colleagues you have allocated to your project may also be working on other projects. Make allowance for this in your scheduling. Furthermore, allow time for approval of the different stages by the decision-making body.

7 Finally, allow for contingency delays – things can go wrong – and for staff holidays, sickness and so on. Base your planning on 40-44 weeks per year (not 52) for productive work.

Setting a schedule means you can see clearly the kind of progress you are making on a project.

Work better

Working effectively is not only a matter of knowing yourself and your work and being organized, and this chapter contains tips on putting in place certain strategies that will enable you to be successful and help you stand out from the crowd. Having clear goals, thinking creatively, being proactive and learning to get things right first time can all be great time-savers, and will help you to work better.

4.1

Work SMART

It is no use having goals that are vague and unrealistic – then, they are more like dreams or aspirations. That may be great for inspiration, but to get things done, you have to be more pragmatic and clear in your mind. Define specific goals to make sure they are realistic and achievable.

A good way to remember this is: goals should be **SMART.**

■ **S = Specific.** Not vague, but clear and precise. State in plain terms what you want to achieve. Focus exactly on what you want to do.

■ **M = Measurable.** The goals should be quantifiable in some way, so that you can assess the progress you are making – or, indeed, not making. You could also build in intermediate steps to fulfilling your overall aim to act as guideposts along the way.

> **case study** Andrew realized that to become fully qualified as an accountant, he needed to study further. The next step for him was to undertake research into the different institutions at which he could study. He had to think whether he had

"The world makes way for the man who knows where he is going"

Ralph Waldo Emerson, American philosopher and essayist

■ **A = Achievable.** You need to focus on goals that are realistic and possible; they should stretch you, but should not be so completely beyond your reach that they are unrealistic and unattainable.

■ **R = Relevant.** Look at the goal in the context of your wider plans. Is it a useful part of the larger vision for what you want to do? Will you be able to put adequate resources into it?

■ **T = Timed.** With a definite time for completion, you can plan interim stages that you'll need to meet. This will help you fulfil your commitment ultimately by beginning to take action right now.

Some authorities also add 'ER' to make it **SMARTER.**

■ **E = Evaluated.** It is important to be able to check on the progress as you move along in order to ensure that you complete your goals.

■ **R = Reported.** It is also useful if the goals are recorded, perhaps at a subsequent meeting or in a report.

Precise goals are easier to keep in sight and focus on clearly.

sufficient funds to pay the fees. He realized that he hadn't, so he had to get a weekend job rather than cut back on other expenses. He was ruthlessly honest and practical, and by setting smart goals he achieved his aim in a few years.

4.2

Spend time to save time

Think of better, more effective ways of working. This will increase the overall efficiency and productivity of your company or organization.

Recently, I was hired as a consultant to look at the organization that dealt with the road-traffic accident-reporting service of the city. I discovered that the engineers who wrote the reports spent a lot of time considering less relevant details of the accidents, such as road surfaces and the conditions of cars, only for those same details to be deleted by a senior engineer who later checked the draft reports.

I suggested that the engineers and senior engineers should meet together at the beginning of the enquiry to decide on the most relevant aspects worth pursuing. The result was increased efficiency: the

case study Sheila was asked to set up a meeting between colleagues in the UK and colleagues in India. She spent a day looking at various options: researching the cost of flights and hotels in the UK, and comparing the cost of hiring videoconferencing facilities. The time Sheila took to investigate

"The reason most goals are not achieved is that we spend our time doing second things first"

Robert J. McKain, inspirational writer

engineers concentrated on the more significant aspects and the senior engineers spent less time deleting unimportant details.

So, stop and think.

■ **Look for the best approach.** Is there a better way than the way you are currently pursuing that will fulfil your overall aims and goals?
■ **Keep your goals in mind.** Don't focus solely on the details of the task; focus on your wider goals and find creative ways of achieving them.
■ **Take time to be efficient.** Your new plan may take time to set up initially, but should ultimately save you time.

Focus on your ultimate overall goal and think of more creative ways in which it could be reached.

different options was well spent: she presented the facts to her boss, and they decided that a meeting by videoconference was the best use of resources. It would mean that colleagues would not have to spend a lot of time travelling, but could talk together in an online virtual conference.

4.3

Be proactive, not reactive

Being proactive means acting responsibly, deciding what you want to do and making certain changes. This is in contrast to being reactive, which we tend to be most of the time: we act according to what has already happened and respond to it.

To be proactive, follow these three main points:

■ **Take responsibility.** Realize that you do not simply have to spend your time 'fire fighting' – that is, responding to crises (probably some of which could have been prevented if there had been better planning). All too often, we're driven by external pressures, and this is an inefficient

case study Shortly after starting to lead seminars on writing clear English, I realized that I needed to branch out, as the market place was crowded with competitors. I discovered that a certain group of managers gained most from my seminars: those who had deliberately chosen a course that didn't

use of our time. Take responsibility for how you spend your time, and if you need to make strategic changes to make yourself more effective, set that as a goal and push for the necessary changes.

■ Think about the implications and effects of your plans. Set some long-term goals and work out how to implement them fully. This means focusing your thoughts and actions on all the aspects of the project over which you have influence. For example, if you are setting up a new accounts system, you need to think about not only all the information that needs to be put into the system, but also all the information that you'll want to derive from it, for reports and so on. Furthermore, you'll need to think about who needs access to the data, and how that might affect the security of the system.

■ Take the initiative. To achieve goals, you'll need to choose a particular path. This may take courage, as you step out into the unknown and perhaps have to face up to colleagues who disagree with your choice of priorities. You may appear confident, but underneath you may be uncertain. Trust yourself and the thorough, constructive work you have put in to make your choices.

Think about how you might change your current practice to become more proactive and in control of your future.

initially involve writing. In particular, I targeted accountants, and currently this is one of my growth areas. The success lay in being proactive: actively deciding upon a new strategy and in formulating a fresh long-term plan to capture a specific sector of the market.

4.4

Identify the important and the urgent

If you make use of an action list (see Secret 3.5), you'll already be in the habit of assessing how urgent and important each task is. Tackle those that are the most urgent and important immediately.

Classify each task by writing a number next to it relating to its importance and urgency – as demonstrated in numbers 1–4 below. Alternatives are to use the letters A to D or different colours. Whichever method you use, what's important is to distinguish:

1 **Urgent and important tasks.** These are the tasks that must be tackled when dealing with a crisis or when a deadline is fast approaching. These are the tasks you must complete first. However, it is troublesome to constantly deal with the urgent and important items; it is better to deal with important items in an ordered, less panicky manner. If an urgent and important task is one that recurs regularly, whether that's every month or once a year, put a note in the diary at an appropriate time in advance of the deadline, so that you can deal with it more efficiently on the next occasion.

2 **Less urgent but important tasks.** Ideally, these tasks should constitute your main workload, so most of your time should be taken up with this level of task. This is the category to tackle after the urgent and important business. They are also associated with fulfilling your long-term goals, including planning and developing relationships.

3 **Urgent but less important tasks.** These may be emailing colleagues, making phone calls or attending a meeting. Reduce these to a minimum, and delegate them if you can.

4 **Least urgent and unimportant items.** Do these in your least productive time. I have a pile of work-related magazines that I look at as I wind down for the weekend on a Friday.

If you don't know where to start on a particular task, start with the part you are least looking forward to tackling, or the part that is most difficult or longest.

Ideally, make sure that most of your time is spent on important but non-urgent tasks – this should be the bulk of your work.

4.5

Break down a task into smaller steps

Breaking a large task down into smaller units can make you feel less afraid or worried about how you are going to tackle it.

If a large task seems hard to grasp and you don't know where to start, create a pattern diagram for it (see Secret 1.2). When you are more certain about the different aspects of the task, break it down into smaller, more manageable steps. Order them into a list that reflects the order in which the actions need to be completed, then create a spreadsheet from that list. If you need to complete certain steps by particular dates, then against each action have a column for: 'Projected date to be completed by'; and another column for: 'Actual date completed by'.

case study Ross had to work out the various stages for his new building project, so he divided the various steps into design and planning, costing, approval by the board and the three phases of completion of the actual project. He entered projected dates for the completion of all tasks onto a spreadsheet so that he could keep track of all the

"Divide each difficulty into as many parts as is feasible and necessary to resolve it"

René Descartes, 17th-century French philosopher

■ **Complete one small step before you go on to the next.** Don't think that working on two or more separate tasks will add variety to your work; it's more likely to just confuse you! Remain focused on, and complete, one action at a time before moving on to the next.

■ **Start with the longest or most difficult.** Unless the actions need to be completed in a particular order, get the most arduous tasks out of the way first. Completing them will give you a psychological boost and a great sense of achievement.

■ **Set a time frame.** Aim to complete a certain number of actions by a particular date or time of day. Enter the date or time they were actually completed on your spreadsheet.

■ **Stop each day's work at a convenient place.** Preferably, you'll get to the end of a particular action, so that you can easily begin a new action on the list when you resume work.

Take control of your work by breaking down a task into manageable steps.

different parts. As he completed his pattern diagram, he realized that he needed to put more effort than he originally thought into communicating the ongoing state of the project to all the staff, suppliers and end users. Analysing the work into smaller steps helped him grasp the details of the whole, and he felt more in control of the project.

4.6

Get it right first time

You may feel that you and your job are unimportant, and that no one values you, but you have a significant part to play in your company or organization. It is important that, whatever you do, you do a good job and carry it out efficiently.

Getting your work right first time, however unimportant it may seem, will save your company or organization time and money. It'll also be beneficial to you, as you won't have the boredom of repeating tasks.

But let's imagine a situation in which you don't get something right. What will happen? Your boss may need to apologize to customers, for example, or call a meeting to discuss ways to remedy the situation, or listen to various members of staff about how to sort out the mess.

case study A certain dry cleaning-company received so many complaints of poor quality cleaning and inadequate customer service that it decided to change its whole approach. Every aspect of the business, from the moment a customer walked into the shop to executive board-room decisions, was examined in great detail to prevent errors

> **"The best preparation for good work tomorrow is to do good work today"** Elbert Hubbard, American artist

Many people would have to spend time putting things right, which would distract them from their main responsibilities, and it would all be because you hadn't fulfilled your role properly.

To instil a 'get it right first time' value in an organization, make sure that every member of staff is aware of the following:

■ The need for quality.
■ That their role and responsibilities are clear to them.
■ That they know exactly what is expected of them.
■ That they will do their best to prevent poor quality.
■ That the cost of poor quality is clearly understood.
■ That their work should be of the utmost quality all the time.
■ That they should think of ways to improve quality further.

Whatever the task, doing it right first time is the most effective use of time.

and bad practices creeping in. Staff were constantly reminded that putting mistakes right cost the company money. Customers received a friendly greeting as they came into the shop and a checklist was instilled in employees to ensure that clothes were always cleaned and returned in top-quality condition.

4.7

Respond creatively to problems

We've all met with occasions when we have come to a stop in our thinking and cannot solve a problem. Time is fast running out and you need to solve the issue quickly and move on. We need to see difficulties and problems as challenges to be tackled.

Here are some creative ways to help you resolve difficulties.

■ **Talk to colleagues.** Talk to them, don't email them. Explain the difficulty to them with as little jargon as possible and as simply as you can. This will encourage you to define the problem and get to its heart. Discuss it, not only to clarify it, but also to work on creative ways to help you through it. Listen to them ... really listen.

■ **Consult an expert.** Ideally, you'll want to talk to someone who has successfully dealt with this kind of problem before. He or she may suggest looking at the matter from an angle that you hadn't thought of.

■ **Think of different ways of describing the difficulty.** Draw the difficulty. Think of a similar way of describing it using art, music or drama. Create an analogy for it. Consult colleagues from different

one minute wonder Think of a metaphor for the problem you're facing. If it's how to increase sales, for example, you might envisage striving to climb a mountain. That might lead you on to think about how you could divide your sales team into those that maintain the base camp and provide support for the elite climbers. The elite would equate to the high flying salespeople, who'd have the goal of reaching the peak. It's a way of thinking through the problem afresh.

backgrounds. Those with a science background may ask more direct or precise questions than those with an arts background, for example.

■ **Give it some deep thought.** Aim at solving the underlying, not the surface, issue. If you are launching a new product, for example, don't just think vaguely about it being successful. Ask yourself, "What would success look like in specific terms?"

■ **Think laterally.** Write a pattern diagram (see Secret 1.2), which will help you think outside the box. A colleague was working on hiring chickens and compiled a pattern diagram to look at various issues. What emerged as the greatest challenge was not any financial aspect but the possible effect on her neighbours. Use a dictionary or thesaurus to generate associated ideas, words and phrases; look also at their opposites.

■ **Take a break.** Sleep on it, if time permits, and come back to it later.

Problem-solving is not all about hard logic. Sometimes you need to be creative in your thinking.

4.8

Life beyond work

Okay, the main focus of this book is on managing your time better at work. But an important part of working well is looking after yourself generally, and that includes taking a break from work: not only pausing in the working day but also relaxing after work, and taking time for holidays.

If you don't take a break, you run the risk of overworking and becoming ill – which would, of course, then interrupt your work. There are two basic spheres of activity that should be part of your life, both to give you a break and for your wider wellbeing. They are:

case study My family and friends told me for years that I was overweight, but I put off doing anything about it. Eventually, I made two decisions: I joined a local gym and enrolled on a slimming class. I confronted my low motivation by asking myself why I had delayed making these decisions. What bothered me was (1) having to spend time

■ **Social activities.** These include spending time with your partner; spending time with family and friends; going to the cinema, theatre or a concert; visiting a museum or art gallery; organizing a charity fun day; or time spent on a hobby such as fishing, gardening or pottery. All these activities help stimulate and entertain the mind.

■ **Physical exercise.** Especially if you work in an office or similarly restrictive environment, exercise is vital for your wellbeing. Things like going for a walk, running, playing sport or working out at a gym help both physically and mentally, by freeing your mind from work.

Schedule these activities into your regular programme – before work, after work or at lunchtime. Despite the fact that taking a lunch break has been proven to increase efficiency, it is often one of the first things to go at busy times.

Another thing to pay attention to is food and drink. Eat a good breakfast and healthy snacks. Avoid too much caffeine and cigarettes, and consider whether you need to cut down on alcohol. Reduce your intake of sugar and fat. Don't eat heavy meals late at night. A healthy diet and lifestyle have a large bearing on how well you perform at work.

Spend some time every day doing something you enjoy.

changing from work to gym clothes and (2) wondering what people would think of me at the gym. I dealt with the first point by working in my gym clothes and the second by telling myself that it was silly to worry about what other people might or might not think. By taking these positive steps my health and general wellbeing have improved.

Work better as a team

Working effectively is not simply a matter of each person working well individually. When people work together, their combined efforts are more beneficial than the sum of their individual results. In a team with good working relationships, each person is clear as to their roles, responsibilities and authority. Tasks are delegated clearly and a balanced team develops, with all members feeling valued and included. This chapter looks at effective teamwork.

5.1

Learn how to manage your boss

Imagine the situation: your boss is hopeless at organization and constantly changes his or her mind about priorities. The instructions they give are not clear and then they raise their voice when they feel you haven't followed their directions.

Alternatively, imagine an opposite scenario: your boss gives you clear instructions but hovers over you to make sure you are carrying out all their wishes. You don't feel trusted to get on with the job. In both these situations, you end up feeling frustrated and not valued.

Our natural tendency is to do what our boss wants or expects, but it's important to learn to manage your boss. Here are some tips:

case study Barry started in a new job and needed to keep asking questions of his manager, Gill. However, Gill was often in meetings and always rushing around. After a while, Gill started replying shortly to Barry's questions by asking him, "What do you think you should do?" This was initially frustrating for

◼ Think about your boss's style of working. Get underneath their surface behaviour patterns and think about them as a person. A good boss will want to get the best out of their staff. Unfortunately, every boss has areas of insecurity and these will become clear over time in a business relationship.

◼ Make it clear that you want to learn. Schedule regular meetings with your boss to review how effectively you have carried out your work.

◼ Ask for clarification. If you're unclear about instructions, ask for clarification. There's no point writing a 20-page report if your boss only wants a 5-page document. This is best done in face-to-face communication, rather than by email. If you ask these questions in an email, you may well go backwards and forwards without making progress.

◼ Agree priorities with your boss. This is particularly true if your boss keeps on piling more and more work on to you. If so, you need to agree the main purpose of your job and the priorities needed to fulfil that purpose. When you have decided these, work out with your boss which of your activities fulfil these priorities and which do not. Then be ruthless: avoid the activities that do not fulfil the agreed priorities.

It is in your boss's interest not to waste your time.

Barry. On the other hand, Gill knew that Barry was gaining experience quickly and was actually closer than her to the situation – and its possible solutions. So, as Barry grew in confidence, he was able to propose his own answers to queries. Gill was then able to effectively ratify Barry's ideas.

5.2

Develop a balanced team

When colleagues work well together as a team, a company or organization can have great impact: they feel involved and are fulfilled, and tasks can be achieved with a great sense of momentum.

Each one of us has our own individual style or working, and a good team will seek to have a balance of various styles. The different styles include colleagues who are able to:

■ **Offer vision.** Some bring lots of ideas and enthusiasm to the team and are able to generate a vision.
■ **Give direction.** Others set the direction to pursue a goal effectively.

case study When Susannah was a customer service manager, she realized that she couldn't possibly do all the work by herself. And so she decided to train up Louise, who seemed eager to learn new skills. Susannah wanted to invest her time and resources in Louise, so that Louise would be confident and equipped to take on more of Susannah's role.

"Coming together is a beginning. Keeping together is progress. Working together is success."

Henry Ford, industrialist

■ **Manage strategy.** You may have colleagues who are great at breaking down a strategy into ordered, manageable tasks.

■ **Manage the logistics.** Others may be more attuned to organizing and managing people, processeses and resources effectively.

■ **Motivate.** It's good to have someone who can motivate colleagues and keep them inspired. They may also identify and develop other colleagues to fufil a vision.

■ **Bring creativity.** New projects especially need creative input from someone with a good imagination.

■ **See a project through.** Every team needs those who excel at completing projects well and to a deadline.

■ **Find solutions.** Someone to steer a way through a crisis.

■ **Build bridges.** Its often important to get people from different backgrounds and disciplines to work together and trust one another.

When colleagues work as a team, everyone's time is used more effectively.

Louise's particular strength was that she was a good listener; she also picked up things that Susannah overlooked. They worked well as a team and, over time, Louise took on increasing responsibilities. When Susannah moved to a different department, Louise was, therefore, able to take over Susannah's role relatively easily.

5.3

Work together harmoniously

In working together as a team, you must clarify roles and responsibilities so that each member of the team knows what he or she is expected to do. This reduces stress and makes for better communication.

Learn to be positive about the various skills and emphases of different members of the team. Attitudes are important. Have respect for one another. Here are a few more pointers for team spirit:

■ **Communicate.** Talk about your joint goals, give clear instructions and explain your actions, so that colleagues can see the bigger picture.

case study Linda is a facilitator and an excellent chairperson. When her company decided to adopt a major new policy, she led an hour-long creative session with the 15 top managers. She put up blank sheets of paper on the wall of the meeting room, with headings of the eight areas the management board had agreed to change. She divided the managers into five groups of three. Each group

■ Clarify roles. Be clear about what authority individuals have.

■ Be positive about colleagues. Take opportunities to affirm one another rather than be critical. Be as positive as you can be.

■ Learn to listen. Respect each team member individually, and recognize that they have a need to express themselves as a unique person.

■ Discuss differences. When problems arise, distinguish details of the incident, the emotions involved and questions of identity that have been raised. Sometimes our assumptions about others' intentions are wrong. If you need to confront a member of the team, do it privately, not publicly. Present criticisms as suggestions or questions if you can.

■ Foster trust. Try to create an environment in which colleagues trust one another and can talk about their development needs.

■ Value different opinions. On minor matters, especially.

■ Don't apportion blame. Blame is unproductive. Instead, identify real issues and seek creative ways of resolving conflict. Be mature. If you've been responsible for a task that's gone well, don't boast about it.

■ Believe in the identity of the team. Remember the acronym TEAM: Together Everyone Achieves More.

In working together as a team, communicate with colleagues as much as you can about your joint goals and aims.

then spent five minutes on each of the eight sheets writing down the activities that they thought needed to be dealt with in that area. The remainder of the session was spent summarizing the results together. Everyone felt the time had been well spent, with all colleagues included and involved. Significant progress was then made in working together to implement the programme for change.

5.4

Delegate effectively

Delegating is the giving of duties, responsibilities or authority to someone so that they can act on your behalf. Many managers are reluctant to delegate, but it is an important way of working effectively and so making better use of everyone's time.

Some managers don't delegate thinking that they are indispensable or even for fear that the colleagues they delegate work to may perform the task better than they themselves can, but this is too narrow-minded. In delegating tasks, you are developing colleagues. This may well increase their motivation and improve their morale: they feel more valued. When delegating, make sure you do the following:

■ **Choose the right people.** Select the personnel you can trust to do the task well. Consider outsourcing or moving non-essential tasks to a different team.

■ **Explain a task clearly.** Give an opportunity for questions. Sometimes you can explain the aims of your task and why you want to achieve it, and you can leave the person you are delegating to work out the best method as to how he or she will do the task.

> "Life is too short to do anything for one's self that one can pay others to do for one"

W Somerset Maugham, British novelist

■ **Discuss possible difficulties.** Think ahead about what problems might be encountered and how they should be approached. This may mean your involvement at key moments in the project.

■ **Provide sufficient resources.** Make sure that the person to whom you have delegated the task has everything they need to be able to perform the task well.

■ **Oversee the work properly.** Set up appropriate arrangements for workers to report back to you and for you to monitor (not interfere with!) the tasks as the work progresses.

■ **Evaluate the work.** At the end of the task, do an evaluation to see how well it went and what could be done differently next time.

It is good to delegate a wide range of tasks, not only the boring or difficult tasks or those that no one really wants to do. Delegating should be about making better use of your time. You can delegate routine tasks, whole projects, or separate parts of a project, so that you can work more effectively. Indeed, it is often said that you should only do the tasks that you cannot delegate. So you should do only the tasks that you alone can do – which may be forward planning, setting priorities and overall management.

Explain a task clearly and give opportunity for questions when you delegate.

5.5

Learn to say "no"

If you say "yes" every time someone asks you to help them with a task, you will never learn to manage your time properly. Part of effective time management is remaining in control of the work you have to do. You therefore need to learn to assert yourself and, at times, say "no".

Saying no is difficult: if we say no, we think we might hurt people's feelings or spoil our chances for the future. But if we don't learn to assert ourselves enough to say no sometimes, we can become stressed all too easily as we take on too many commitments and cannot do all the tasks to the best of our ability. Here are some guidelines on how to assert yourself:

case study Bill felt pleased that he had been asked to speak at the conference. At last he was becoming recognized! The only difficultly was the conference was scheduled for the time his wife was expecting their second child. So he faced a dilemma: to speak at the conference and not be there for his wife and family; or to be with his wife

■ Be clear about your own priorities and goals. Does the task being suggested fit in with the priorities and goals you have set yourself? If it does, then consider it; if it doesn't, reject it.

■ Think about the effects of taking on a further task. Would you have to delay completing other tasks? What would be the result for your wider life?

■ Learn to be fair to yourself as well as to others. Realize you have a right to say no. You do not have to accept everything that comes your way, and you have a right to express your own point of view.

■ Assert yourself firmly and positively. Suggest other choices that the other person could follow up. Don't apologize. Learn to be firm and direct, not aggressive or timid. Practise making such statements as, "I'd love to be involved that afternoon, but I've already got plans"; "It's nice to be asked, but I can't help you at the moment"; and "I need to check my diary – ask me again later" (not: "I'll come back to you later", as that would put a burden on you).

If your boss is asking you to take on another task, remember that you can put the responsibility for the decision back on him or her by saying, "Well, this is what I'm working on at the moment – which do you want me to do?"

You do not have to accept everything that comes your way.

and family and miss out on a good opportunity to speak at the conference? In the end, he chose to stay with his wife. He explained the reasons to the conference organizers, who were impressed with his decisions on work-life balance. They assured him they would approach him again for the next conference a few months later, which they did.

5.6

Plan better meetings

Work out the aims of your meeting. Are you having a meeting just because you have always had one? Are you even having a meeting to discuss other meetings?

The purposes of meetings can be any or all of the following: to inform, to discuss and to decide.

■ **To inform.** To brief participants on progress reports, for example; to communicate information, perhaps on trends or industry news; or maybe just to motivate colleagues.

■ **To discuss.** To negotiate a contract or finalize arrangements for a project or new initiative; to talk through the various aspects of an issue, such as the profitability of plans or some other financial issue; to resolve an area of conflict that has arisen.

one minute wonder Work out how much your meetings cost. Look back at Secret 1.4 and calculate your hourly rate with overheads. If it is £50, for example, multiply that by the number of colleagues at a meeting and the number of hours it lasts. A three-hour meeting would thus cost your company £900 – quite possibly a lot more than you thought!

"Meetings are a symptom of bad organization. The fewer meetings the better" Peter F. Drucker, management theorist

■ **To decide.** To make a decision on the next steps that the organization needs to take or which new projects should be pursued; or to formulate action points that colleagues are to follow up.

Prepare for a meeting in this way:

■ **Work out the practicalities.** Matters such as participants, start and finish times and the venue.

■ **Prepare a specific agenda.** Give a clear focus to the agenda. Don't simply put "Next year's exhibition"; put "Next year's exhibition: aims; lessons from last year; practicalities".

■ **Order the agenda.** Put the more important parts of the agenda early on in the meeting. Don't be tempted to put the less significant, more administrative items early on – you may well get sidetracked by people raising minor details leaving less time for the big topics.

■ **Plan ahead.** Work through in advance possible objections that might be raised that would prevent goals from being fulfilled. Discuss controversial items in advance with the relevant people concerned.

■ **Schedule the attendance.** If certain people need to be present only for particular parts of a meeting, arrange that in advance.

■ **Get the reading done beforehand.** Circulate brief (maximum one-page) reports in advance, so as not to waste precious time during the meeting while colleagues read the report.

It is crucially important to know why you are holding a meeting.

5.7

Run better meetings

Even if a meeting has been well planned, it may not be effective. Colleagues may arrive late or not turn up: discussion may be unfocused or not constructive; motivation may be generally poor. How do you transform such a situation?

A good chairperson will lead a meeting well. He or she will involve others, being both tactful and firm and not allowing only a few colleagues to take part in the discussion. He or she will also summarize progress by restating important points and give a lead, knowing when to conclude discussion, call for a decision and move on to the next point. A good chairperson will also be clear on the action points.

case study Julie was called in to sort out the poor organization of a committee. She immediately noticed that participants didn't arrive on time. To solve this, she would start a meeting at the arranged time, even if there was only one other person there; the others quickly got the message. She also noticed that no proper agendas were circulated in advance. Colleagues just came to the meeting and

In a good meeting, all colleagues participate. Some meetings are poor because everyone is waiting for others to say something. I believe each participant has an important role to play. Here is a checklist of points to remember in taking an active part in meetings:

- Listen to the point of view expressed by others.
- Be clear in your comments.
- Define roles and responsibilities as necessary.
- Be prepared to change your mind.
- Be positive and open-minded.
- Clarify issues if you are unsure.
- Confront issues, not the person expressing an issue.
- Stay focused.

It is important that at a meeting everyone should agree who will follow up with further action, what action that person should take and a time by which it should be completed. Action points should be SMARTER (see Secret 4.1). See also the advice on note taking and writing minutes (Secret 6.7).

Ensure that your meetings always start and finish on time.

asked, "What do we need to discuss?". Consequently, discussion wandered, with no clear focus. Julie appointed a chairperson to solve this. She also realized that no action points were agreed at the end of a meeting, so she introduced a clear follow-through procedure so that the action points could be evaluated at the beginning of the next meeting. The result: a smoothly running committee.

Communicate more effectively

We live in an age of instant communication and email is the most frequently used form. It is not always the best form of communication, though. Sometimes a phone call or talking face to face with a colleague is more effective. The secret is knowing why you are communicating. To just check facts or to build a relationship? In this chapter, you'll need to focus on how you use the various tools of communication and learn how to be a more effective communicator.

6.1

Think about how you communicate

Most communication in offices these days is through the form of email. It is important to consider other ways of communicating: face to face and the phone.

Here are some of advantages and disadvantages of each form:

■ **Email.** *Advantages:* It's fast, gives a permanent record, works across time zones, can have data attached easily, can communicate to many people. *Disadvantages:* It does not build relationships as well as more direct communication. It is also not good for dealing with sensitive issues.

■ **Telephone.** *Advantages:* It is more personal than email, illicits an immediate response, is good for developing a rapport and allows you to explain your message further if necessary. *Disadvantages:* You can't communicate easily to a large group of people, and it cannot be used throughout the day across all time zones.

case study Sandeep uses his Blackberry a lot. It's ideal, as he travels extensively, and he can receive all his emails and phone calls at one point, and text friends and colleagues easily. The only problem is

◄ Face-to-face. *Advantages:* This form is the most helpful for giving bad news or discussing sensitive information. Likewise when you need to impart important information and when you need to see someone's response. *Disadvantages:* It may be expensive in terms of time spent.

Certain kinds of communication should be handled in certain ways:

◄ When arranging a date for a meeting, phone the one or two people you definitely want at the meeting to get a choice of two (or a maximum of three) potential dates. Then email others to see who can come on those dates.

◄ When making contact with a new client, phone or email to make an appointment for a face-to-face meeting so that you can build a good working relationship.

◄ If you're asking colleagues for comments on a draft proposal by email, state when you want their comments back by.

◄ To confirm details agreed in a phone conversation, it is best done by email, but to make a legal agreement that both parties have to sign, then a letter is best.

◄ If you need to explain to your boss why a project is delayed, that is best done in a face-to-face meeting.

Email is efficient, but may not always be the best way to communicate.

knowing when to switch it off, as it can control his life – and that of his partner too. He now disciplines himself to switch it off when he gets off the train at the end of his evening commute.

6.2

Cope with email

In the last few years, email has revolutionized the way in which we communicate around the world. It's cheap, fairly reliable and, above all, it's fast. But how can we cope with the email inbox?

You will be distracted from your present task if you constantly check emails, so schedule certain times of the day to open and respond to them. Don't always give in to the pressure to reply immediately.

Here are 10 commandments of email use:

1 Make the subject line clear: this will help your reader see what you are writing about and how important it is.

2 Include a greeting and close. Having no greeting and/or sign-off is unfriendly. There is no fixed etiquette: the style of greeting in emails is more informal than a letter but putting "Hi Adam" to someone you have not dealt with before is too too casual. Set up your email signatures with a range of phrases you frequently use, such as "Good to have met you on…" and "I look forward to hearing from you". Include contact information (phone number, address etc) in your 'signature'.

3 Only send copies to those who really need to see the email: keep to a minimum the number of people you send copies to.

4 Work out what you want to be the response to your email. Is it clear? Do you want them to reply or not? If you do, by when?

5 In long emails, give particular attention to the information that appears on the opening screen. Your reader will use that as a basis for deciding whether to scroll down further or not.

6 Be careful to use the appropriate tone. One of the disadvantages of email is that the words can seem abrupt. You may need to soften the tone to build a relationship with your reader.

7 Don't be careless: email is no excuse for inaccurate grammar, spelling or punctuation.

8 Take care over presentation. Email doesn't mean that you can write in long rambling sentences without proper paragraphs. Think clearly; draft the text, then go back over it to revise it. For important communications, print the text and read it on hard copy, as you will spot more errors that way.

9 Use only abbreviations that are generally known, not obscure ones that may be perceived as jargonistic.

0 Avoid capitals: these indicate SHOUTING and should always be avoided. An email is not the place to be emotional.

earn to control your use of emails.

6.3

Speak on the phone

Rather than emailing, I prefer to use the telephone if I want to build a business relationship with a colleague in a different organization. The tone of their voice comes over in a phone conversation and I can explain something more easily if I sense that the other person hasn't understood what I have said.

Remember that phone calls require preparation, though. Make a list of the relevant points you want to discuss or confirm before you call your colleague. As you finish your call, agree and summarize the action points, such as who will do what and by when: "So you're okay to let me have the details by the end of the week?"

Make a note to file of the key points, and, if important, confirm what you have agreed in an email. Your note to file could be a hard copy in your project file, it could be made electronically on your computer, or could simply be jotted down in your diary – something such as to check at the beginning of the following week that details were sent, and, if not, to chase up that task.

When speaking on the phone, I sometimes ask, "Is now a convenient time to speak?" If it isn't, then I arrange to speak at a different time that is more convenient to them. I've even jokingly begun by saying, "Please excuse this old-fashioned form of communication." It's

one minute wonder When making a call, always be prepared to leave a message on an answerphone. Speak more slowly than you would normally; state your name and succinctly explain why you are phoning. Then leave your contact details so the other person can call you back without having to search for your number. It's surprising how often this is forgotten.

a bit of levity, and also tests the water on whether the call has caught them at a bad moment or busy time. If you sense it has, stay in control of the situation and offer to call them back at a more convenient time.

When speaking to a colleague on the phone, put points across and listen to the response of the other person. If you detect hesitation, you can offer to explain the point again or expand upon it to clarify.

If you are making an arrangement on the phone, minimize further phone calls by saying something such as, "Let's leave it that we'll meet at 3pm unless I ring to say otherwise". This means that you would only have to make a further phone call if the arrangement changed, not simply to confirm it.

Key points when communicating by phone:

■ Prepare the points or questions you want to make beforehand.
■ After the call, make a note of the key points that were covered.
■ Check that everything's clearly understood during the conversation and agree actions to be taken if required.
■ If you are calling to set up a meeting, decide on all the arrangements rather than necessitating a further call to confirm the venue etc.

Prepare for an important phone call by writing down in advance the relevant points you want to discuss.

6.4

Make better use of your computer

Your computer is more than a typewriter. It contains useful tools that will save you time. Learn what those are to make better use of your time.

■ **Track changes.** Use the 'track changes' facility to correct work so that it is clear who has made corrections.

■ **Create templates.** Do this for work that you undertake regularly.

■ **Make files easy to find.** For example, I work on some projects for the publisher Zondervan. But I give these the file name "azondervan" so that it is alphabetically nearer the top of my root directory to save me time when I want to open it.

■ **Use coordinated software.** Outlook or similar software is able to coordinate your email, calendar, contacts, etc.

case study I'm a great believer in 'tools auto correct' – a facility that automatically corrects a word that you have keyed in wrongly: "abbout" to "about", for example. I used it when I edited a 9-million word reference book. As I set up the project, I knew that I'd be keying in very common English words many

one minute wonder On PCs, shift F3 will change all caps to lowercase or initial caps: useful if you've left the 'caps lock' key on by mistake: highlight the words and press shift F3. Shift F7 will give you a list of synonyms (thesaurus) – this is a more extensive listing than is available by just right-clicking the mouse.

■ **Create macros.** A macro is a group of computer commands that can be set up to be performed automatically by a single click. It saves time for tasks that you perform frequently.

■ **Back up your data.** Make sure you do this regularly (if this is not done automatically by your office). Test the backup periodically and actually restore data to make sure your system works.

■ **Set automatic reminders.** For any regular tasks, from undertaking reviews, to paying bills, to remembering important birthdays, setting automated reminders is a great help.

If you're not sure of any of these time savers, ask a colleague or your IT department for help. Also consider investing in new software, as long as it will genuinely help you work more effectively.

Learn to use your computer fully to save time and work more effectively.

times. So I looked at a list of the 100 most common words and devised shorter forms that would be auto-corrected. "Because" was "bec", "would" was "wd" and "the" was merely "t". I reckon I saved myself several weeks of keyboarding time simply by developing these short forms.

6.5

Make the most of the Internet

The Internet has revolutionized much of life, in both business and social settings. Access to the Internet is generally very widely available and is relatively cheap. It can save time in many ways – but, be warned, it can also be one of the biggest time-wasters.

Because of the speed of access to a vast array of data, the Internet offers many ways to save you time. Just make sure you use it in a way that's beneficial to you and your company. Here are some of ways in which you can use the Internet to save time.

■ **Carrying out research.** Its great for looking up information on companies or organizations, for checking facts via sites such as

case study In networking, Karl knows that the Internet is useful to gain background information, but he also regularly attends real-life networking events, where he can meet new business contacts face to face. By checking out websites and

Wikipedia, and for finding out the times of trains, buses or planes when organizing trips. Before the arrival of the Internet, a reference library was one of the key places where information could be found. But going there took time, its hours of opening were limited, and finding the right piece of information could mean reading through several publications.

■ **Buying goods or services.** Online shopping is another obvious time-saver – or at least it can be. The saving is in the time you would otherwise have spent trudging round the shops. However, online shopping isn't the place for browsing. Target what you want to buy, then use the search facilities and consumer forums to find the best product, price and service.

■ **Obtaining news updates.** For global news, checking financial markets or keeping abreast of changing conditions in your particular sphere of business, the Internet has become indispensable.

■ **Communicating and networking.** As well as emailing colleagues and friends (see Secret 6.2), the Internet is being used increasingly for online social and business networking sites, such as Facebook and LinkedIn. The work-related sites can be useful for developing and maintaining business contacts. It's a way of finding out who's working where and on what projects, and of communicating to others about you and your business.

The Internet is a wonderful resource, but make sure you don't spend more time on it than is necessary.

professional networking sites in advance, he finds out all he can about an organization or a person before he actually meets them. In this way, he prepares himself to ask intelligent questions about them at his meetings.

6.6

Listen carefully

The art of listening to others is often neglected as a communication skill. Yet it is vitally important, to make the most effective use of time and to help reduce problems of misunderstanding.

What do I mean by good listening?

1 Respect each individual as distinct; recognize they have a need and a right to express themselves as a unique person.

2 Focus on the other person; look at them. Very often in conversations, while the other person is talking, we are thinking about what we can say in response to them rather than actually listening to them. Good listening strengthens relationships.

3 Listen to the words that other people say, of course, but go beyond that: notice their tone, expressions and pauses; be aware of their feelings, and notice, too, what's not said.

4 Understand other people. We can only do this effectively, though, if we are confident in ourselves, rather than, for example, worrying about what people are thinking about us.

"A wise old owl lived in an oak,
The more he saw the less he spoke,
The less he spoke the more he heard.
Why can't we all be like that wise
old bird?" **Traditional nursery rhyme**

5 Respect people's privacy and don't delve more deeply into a subject than a person wants to disclose.

6 Listen out for cues that people want to express more of themselves, then respond accordingly – perhaps by a short "mmm", which expresses the wish to allow the other person to say more, or a short questions to prompt them to continue. An acquaintance once said to me, "I've been really unhappy since my wife died". I gently responded, "When was that?" He told me it was 12 years before and then talked for a long time about her. I was aware of his desire to talk and responded to his cue.

7 Reflect back – that is summarize in a few words – what the person has been saying. This shows that you are really listening and trying to understand. They will soon put you right if you've misunderstood.

Good listening strengthens relationships and reduces the likelihood of time-consuming misunderstandings.

6.7

Make good notes

You make notes to record the main points of a text, presentation, or the decisions made at a meeting or during a phone conversation so that they are an accurate record that you can go back to later.

There are three ways of making notes:

■ **Write an organized logical list of points under headings.**
Number the various different points. Note key words. Write in phrases, not sentences. Invent your own abbreviations and use them. I have followed this method over the years, and I always copy up my notes later. It's time-consuming but has helped me greatly. I have found that, in the process of making a more ordered copy of my rough notes, I have the opportunity to digest what I have written earlier.

case study Part of Annie's job was to take minutes of a meeting. The chairwoman of the committee, Sandra, was good at stating clearly the decisions the committee agreed and Annie knew she had to record them accurately. During the actual meetings, Annie took notes of the decisions, keyboarded them up neatly later and passed them to Sandra for

■ **Underline or highlight phrases in a text.** Do this either in your own copy of a book or a photocopy. Mark key phrases, write questions in the margin and use wavy lines to indicate points you disagree with.

■ **Complete a pattern diagram of what you have understood.** When reading a text or attending a meeting, make a word diagram (see Secret 1.2) of the sense you have grasped from the points discussed.

Whichever methods you adopt, your main aim is to record the important points (not every part) of what you are reading or listening to. If you are taking minutes of a meeting, you need to record who will undertake a particular action, and when it is to be completed (see Secret 4.1 on setting SMART goals). If you are quoting exact words, then make sure you record them accurately with the precise source. I sometimes also put my own thoughts in square brackets.

Have questions in your mind when listening or reading:

- What point is the author making?
- What is this really about?
- Why is this important?

Note-making is a powerful key to understanding.

final approval before circulating them. Annie found it difficult to record notes of a disagreement but found it helpful to use the expression, "There was some disagreement with this view and the following comments were made", followed by an objective, bullet-point list of the comments. Annie was praised for the clarity of her minutes.

6.8

Read more quickly

Reading is part of the process of communication: you want to absorb written material as efficiently and effectively as possible. It is important to decide why you are reading something – do you want to extract certain specific information from a website, article or book? Will you be asked questions about what you are reading? Will you have to write about it?

After you have decided why you are reading a text, consider how much time you want to set aside for reading. Do you have only a few brief minutes and need to locate a specific point in detail or do you want to read a piece of writing for its wider points of discussion?

■ **Seeking out a specific detail.** First check to see if the text has a list of contents or an index that you can use to locate what you are looking for. If it is a report, check to see whether it has an executive summary (an overall summary of the whole report) or conclusions. Also, pay particular attention to the beginning and ends of chapters, and, within that, sections and paragraphs. If the text is well written, you should be able to tell what the paragraph is about from its first sentence.

"Reading is to the mind what exercise is to the body"

Joseph Addison, 18th-century English essayist

■ **Learning the art of skim reading.** If you want to understand a text in terms of its wider points of discussion but are pushed for time, bear in mind that you don't have to read every word. Instead, focus your eyes on groups of words, and especially on the main content words (nouns and verbs), rather than on function words such as 'a', 'the', 'of' and 'for'. Don't stop and look up every word you don't know in a dictionary. Only do that with what seem to be important words.

■ **Absorbing the arguments.** If you are going to have to answer questions on, or write about, what you have read, take notes on the text. Making notes will help you take in the text and make it part of your thinking. Making notes could include paraphrasing (putting in your own words) what the author is saying or quoting the author's actual words. If you do the latter, make sure you note the page number, website, etc accurately.

After you have finished reading, you can think about what the text said. Ask yourself these questions about its meaning:

■ Did you agree with the text? If not, why not?
■ Would you have expressed things differently? If so, in what way?

Don't think you have to read every word of a document. Learn techniques that help you grasp its overall sense.

6.9

Think about what you're writing

Emails and other forms of written communications are often muddled and unclear. This means that the person reading them must spend extra time trying to work out what you are attempting to say. To make the best use of your reader's time, think carefully about what you want to communicate.

Here are some points to think about when you plan to write an email, letter or report; they are grouped in the acronym **AIR**:

■ **A = Audience.** Think about who you are writing to. How much does your reader know about the subject you are writing about? You will write in different styles, depending on your audience: for example the

one minute wonder Take a report that you have written. Print it out, and read it through. Are your key messages crystal clear? What response do you want from your readers? Is that clearly stated? Revise it till you are 100% happy with it.

> "The time to begin writing an article is when you have finished it to your satisfaction. By that time you begin to clearly and logically perceive what it is you really want to say"

Mark Twain, American author

way in which you write to your boss or the managing director will be different from the way you write to your colleague at the next desk.

■ **I = Intention.** Ask yourself what message you want to communicate. Think carefully about the central part of what you want to say. What are its key messages? Do you need to explain some background or give some context before you can get to what you really want to say? Use standard paragraphs for parts of a text you write often, or cut and paste from other documents, but always use these only as a basis for the document you are composing. Check that the text absolutely applies to the particular document you are writing.

■ **R = Response.** What response are you expecting from your communication? What do you want your reader to do with your message? On one of my writing courses, the response that a colleague wanted was buried in brackets towards the end of a 79-word sentence! If the response you want your readers to make isn't clear to you, then it certainly won't be clear to them.

Every time you are about to write a document, think AIR.

6.10

Write more clearly

If you write clearly, you will make the best use of your reader's time. He or she will not need to read your email or report several times to understand what you are saying, so it's an important skill to develop.

Here's the **ABC** of clarity in your communications:

■ **A = Accurate.** Check your facts, and recheck them. We've all been invited to meetings on Wednesday 1 December, when in fact 1 December is a Tuesday: did the writer mean Wednesday 30 November or Thursday 1 December? And so time is wasted with emails flying backwards and forwards simply because the original writer didn't bother to check a calendar. Be as precise and unambiguous as possible. Use standard English grammar and correct punctuation and spelling. If in doubt, check, and don't rely just on your computer's spell check facility; it won't pick up on the wrong use of a word, such as mistaking "loose" and "lose" or typing "fiend" instead of "friend".

■ **B = Brief.** Some people tend to ramble, expressing the same thought in different ways throughout a text. Others are too concise and simply write their 15 words and then wonder why the world hasn't changed. To both I say: ask yourself, who?, why?, what?, where?, when? and how?

"I didn't have time to write a short letter, so I wrote a long one instead"

Mark Twain, American author

Those who tend to ramble will find the discipline of answering these questions particularly useful in the editing stage. After having drafted a text, go back over it, answering each of these questions. You may well find that you have answered them at various points throughout your text. Cut and paste the relevant sections and edit them to present a more ordered argument. Those who are too brief will find that answering these questions expands their argument, giving it greater depth.

■ **C = Clear.** To make the best use of your reader's time, your aim should be for him or her to be able to understand immediately what you are trying to communicate the first time they read your text. All too often, a writer just puts down thoughts in no particular order, creating hurdles that, figuratively speaking, a reader has to jump over to try and understand a document. Expressing yourself clearly is largely the result of clear thinking and arranging the text in a logical, ordered way.

Spend time to make your documents as clear as possible, so that they make the best use of your reader's time.

Take control of your time

There is a range of different techniques to help you manage your working time more effectively. They include creating blocks of time within your schedule for completing a task so that you gather momentum in your work; undertaking forward planning to reduce future problems; staying concentrated and focused; setting in place arrangements to help you minimize interruptions; and making good use of any slack time that arises unexpectedly.

7.1

Create blocks of time

It can be very useful to create blocks of time when you perform different tasks. This is especially useful for the main work you need to do, but is also useful for more routine tasks.

For example, you may need to compile a weekly sales report on a Tuesday, referring to the previous week's sales. So, set aside time every Monday to speak to colleagues in the Sales Department and also to make sure that the figures provided on your computer system are accurate. Then, every Tuesday, allocate a block of time for actually writing your report. These are the priority tasks every Monday and Tuesday that you should not be distracted from.

Blocking time out in your diary for these tasks saves you from working on them only when you feel like it.

Here are some further tips for managing your time during periods of concentrated work:

one minute wonder Consider blocking time in your diary for making phone calls, taking into account the best time to get in touch with people. It can be a more efficient use of time than an ad hoc approach.

"Work expands so as to fill the time available for its completion"

Parkinson's Law, written by C. Northcote Parkinson, London 1955

■ **Disconnect yourself.** If at all possible, turn off your mobile device, close your email application, and put your phone on answerphone (with the volume off). If you really need to concentrate, see if you can go to a different office space where nobody will disturb you.

■ **Learn to squeeze time.** Set yourself a limit of, say, 30 minutes and then stretch yourself to see if you can fit in, say, 40 minutes' work: you may be surprised to see that you do actually fit that in. This works the other way, too: a meeting scheduled to last 90 minutes will tend to last that long, as the quote above attests. See if you can reduce it by 10 or even 15 minutes.

■ **Give yourself a break.** After 50 minutes' concentrated work, give yourself a ten-minute break: this will allow your mind to process and digest your thoughts, and you may find yourself solving some of the problems raised during your time of concentrated action.

Working in blocks of time creates its own momentum that enables you to work more effectively.

7.2

Stay focused

Aim to give your complete attention to the task you are dealing with currently, so that you complete it well. Stay focused and concentrate on reaching a goal and achieving a particular result.

This may mean that, rather than saying to yourself that you will work for two hours on a report before you go home, you instead say, "I will complete the actual writing of the first two sections of the report". Here are some more basic rules to maintain a focus on your time.

■ **Give yourself realistic deadlines.** If you don't give yourself a deadline, you risk wasting your time, so be firm with yourself and stretch yourself slightly, but don't be unrealistic or overdemanding. When setting a deadline, learn from previous experience. For instance,

case study The Club's committee realized they were working inefficiently and, when Ed took over as chairperson, he decided to make changes. The committee members used to talk about important issues such as finance and future policy, but the time was wasted because they never pursued the subjects fully and never reached any conclusions.

I keep a file called 'Project Analyses'. At the end of each project, I compare my costings and time actually spent with the costings and time I thought would be needed at the outset. I use this when looking at similar future projects to estimate the resources I need.

■ **Learn to deal effectively with interruptions.** If you are interrupted in your work, try to complete the immediate aspect of the work (such as keying in a column of figures). Sometimes I say to someone who interrupts me, "Do you mind if I finish writing this sentence?" Before you go to lunch or at the end of the day, write yourself a brief note about where you had got up to and any thoughts you have on the next step. This will help you get back into the work after your break.

■ **Control your communications.** If you communicate with a colleague frequently, build up a list of the items you need to discuss or keep adding them to one draft email, rather than sending a series of emails or making several phone calls, which is an inefficient use of time. Try to be more structured in your methods by, say, arranging to speak on the phone at a particular time on a certain day of the week.

Avoid distractions and focus on getting things done to achieve more.

Ed decided he'd ask one committee member to prepare a discussion paper on future policy to be distributed in advance of the next meeting. The paper listed options for the future direction of the club, with firm action points. By preparing the ground beforehand, the meetings of the committee were much more focused and productive.

7.3

Keep your paperwork under control

If you keep dealing with pieces of paper without making a definite decision as to what to do with them, you're wasting time. As far as possible, make sure that you deal only once with a piece of paper that comes across your desk.

So when you pick up a document, get into the habit of dealing with it in one of the following ways:

■ **Bin it.** Throw away junk mail. Throw away papers you have dealt with and no longer need. Resist the temptation to file many of them. Recycle non-confidential paper, but shred confidential documents, such as invoices and legal or tax documents.

case study Jack used to complain about the amount of post he had to deal with, but he was really using it as a distraction from his work. I pointed this out to him and got him to be more disciplined with the post. Now, when it comes in each day, Jack puts half of it – especially advertising and marketing

■ **Deal with it.** This might involve reading it or replying to it – one way is to write in hand on the document and return it to the sender. If the document is important, then you can make a note in your action list to come back to it at a more convenient time – time that you have specially alloted for this task. Or the paper might remind you to phone or email a colleague – if so, enter the details on your action list and keep the relevant piece of paper close to hand.

■ **File it.** File important documents, but resist the habit of filing documents just in case you will need them. Only file documents that you are sure you will need (such as invoices, contracts and tax information). Regularly go through your filing cabinets, throwing away papers that you no longer need. Don't ask yourself, "Would it be nice to keep this?" but rather, "Have I got to keep this?"

As far as possible, you should aim to deal only once with a piece of paper when it comes across your desk.

pamphlets – straight to recycling or in the wastepaper bin. He sets aside a small portion of the post to read later at a time he's blocked off in his diary and replies immediately to minor administrative requests that come in. In this way, he finds he can now keep right on top of his paperwork.

7.4

Use slack time well

We all have occasional slack periods of time. They could be anything from a few minutes to a few hours to several days, but, however short the time frame, the secret is to learn to use such periods effectively.

The first point is to anticipate and prepare yourself for slack periods. They may come when you're outside a colleague's office waiting for him or her to become available, when you arrive early for a meeting, when you're delayed on a train, when your computer or printer is being very slow, or when you're waiting for your phone call to be answered by the right person. If you're thinking ahead, you'll be ready to make the most of such moments.

Here are some ways in which you can usefully take advantage of these kind of times:

■ **Make routine phone calls.** Keeping in touch with colleagues, finding out the progress of a project, making sure that someone is carrying out a task or possibly checking on payments.

■ **Catch up on answering emails.** If you're on the move or otherwise out of the office, you'll need to use a laptop or a device such as a Blackberry or iPhone for this.

■ Read a report. Make sure it's not confidential, though. I was once on a train and sat down next to a man working on a police report. When I asked him about how life was as a police officer, he genuinely asked how I knew he was a member of the police. I just pointed out, "It says on your file 'Police report'"!

■ Tidy papers or archive your files. A good use of time if you're in the office, though you could clear files on your laptop too.

■ Check through notes. Read through notes of meetings, conversations and so on. You could order and write them up too.

■ Read a business book or journal. We're often too busy to do as much reading as we'd like, and a period of slack time is perfect for catching up on work-related reading.

■ Read a non-work-related book or magazine. Conversely, reading something that's not work-related can free the mind and possibly help with your lateral thinking.

■ Solve a problem. This could be a difficulty at work or something entirely abstract, such as a crossword or sudoku puzzle.

■ Go for a walk. Any form of exercise would be a good use of time, but walking is particularly good for helping people think.

■ Delete old messages on your mobile. Okay, not much fun, but it needs to be done and this could be the best time for doing it.

The main lesson here is to expect delays and spare moments and to prepare for them. I often travel by train to lead courses and I always take with me work for an extra two hours beyond my journey time, in case of delays. And I always take a pen and paper with me.

Always be prepared to find good uses for the odd slack periods of time that unexpectedly come your way.

7.5

Deal with interruptions

We all have interruptions at work that slow us down or distract us from the task in hand. We need to learn how to deal with them to minimize their effects.

Here are some guidelines to help you deal better with interruptions to your working day:

■ **Don't distract yourself.** Be disciplined and exercise self-control. Don't check your emails constantly, for example, or make a call as soon as the idea pops into your head. If you do, your productivity will decrease. Schedule in particular times of the day for these routine tasks.

case study If colleagues call by Peter's desk, he has learnt not to invite them to sit down, so that they don't linger. He knows its better to arrange a time to meet them later: "Joe, let's catch up over a sandwich at lunch time, shall we?" The managers in the office where Peter worked arranged the office furniture so that it does not invite people to sit

■ Be proactive. If someone emails you and asks when he or she can speak to you on the phone, take control and tell them the best time, giving a narrow time slot: "I'm free between 4.20 and 4.30 pm today".

■ Be clear with instructions. When you're giving instructions to a colleague you have delegated work to, make your instructions crystal clear, so they don't constantly need to ask for advice. And when someone comes to you asking for help, ask him or her how they might solve the problem for themselves – that will save you time later, as they'll have learnt how, and have confidence, to solve problems themselves.

■ Delegate to trusted colleagues. Give responsibility and authority to colleagues you trust most, and accept that their style of working might be different to yours. Don't interfere unless you have to.

■ Take control. Try to schedule dealing with an interruption at a time to suit you: "Let's talk about this at 4 o'clock". If that is not possible, tell them you've got five minutes now (reply with a relatively short time). Finish your immediate task, such as writing a sentence or adding up a column of figures, to minimize the effect of the interruption.

■ Be assertive: learn to say no sometimes. On occasions, "no" is the only reasonable reply if you are to work effectively in your role.

As far as you can, be proactive in arranging your working environment so that you minimize interruptions.

down and chat. When Peter has work that requires intense concentration, he screens incoming calls and switches his phones off, telling colleagues that he is not to be disturbed for a period of time. Sometimes he finds a quiet corner in the office to finish a report, and occasionally works from home to restrict possible interruptions further.

7.6

Combat tiredness

However well you learn to manage your time, there are occasions for all of us when our workload demands that we dig deep and carry on that little bit further. When a tight deadline must be met, for example, or to cope with an unexpected event, such as illness of a work colleague. At times like this, we may need to work long hours and keep our focus, despite the effects of tiredness.

So, how do you combat fatigue when you have competing demands on your time, yet your eyelids are starting to drop and your mind is starting to wander? Here are some pointers to juggling intense periods of work and the effects of tiredness. But be warned: these are measures to cope with temporary fatigue and should not be applied over prolonged periods, which could have serious health consequences.

■ **Don't overuse caffeine.** When we're tired and still need to work, one of the first things we often reach for is a strong tea or coffee. This is a very temporary fix, though, and overuse can cause a jitteriness.
■ **Drink water.** Dehydration will contribute to fatigue, so keep drinking water regularly throughout the day.

"More men are killed by overwork than the importance of the world justifies" Rudyard Kipling, English author

■ **Take breaks.** Even when we're at our busiest, our minds and bodies need breaks. Remember, you'll work more effectively after a break, so don't feel guilty about taking one. Walk, run or put your feet up and close your eyes for 20 minutes or so. Listen to your body's demands.

■ **Relax before sleeping.** An intense work situation can adversely affect our sleep – we can go to bed exhausted, yet be unable to get off to sleep, our minds still whirring. What you need to do is spend about 30 minutes before going to bed relaxing deeply. That's not watching TV or reading, but controlling and calming the mind and body.

■ **Keep exercising.** We sometimes feel as if there isn't enough time to exercise when we're busy, but this is precisely the time when it is most beneficial. A vigorous exercise session will give your mind something else to focus on and will stretch out those knotted muscles.

■ **Utilize your most productive time wisely.** If you followed Secret 1.3, you'll know your best time in the day for working. Try to use this period for the most challenging tasks.

■ **Use lists.** As mentioned throughout this book, it's important to break down work into manageable tasks. Use lists for this, so you can tick off completed tasks and get a sense of progress and achievement.

■ **Share the workload.** A heavy load is always easier when it's shared, so delegate even small tasks wherever you can. It'll help create a team sensibility – a feeling of all pullling together – and so is great for morale. And keep in close contact with colleagues to share your burdens rather than bottling them up and internalizing the stress.

Exercise regularly, take breaks and drink plenty of water to beat fatigue.

7.7

Put it all into practice

The aim throughout this book has been to help you work not only efficiently, but also effectively.

Here are some final words of encouragement to help you make the most of your time:

■ **Set priorities.** Set certain priorities in your life, and develop plans that derive from them. Separate planning from doing.

■ **Conquer large and complicated tasks.** Divide large tasks into smaller, more manageable parts. Work on one of these at a time and do it to the best of your ability.

■ **Be organized.** Use files and archives (electronic or hard copy) effectively, by clearly labelling and ordering them; set up systems for routine tasks. And do simple things, such as putting things back in the right place when you have finished with them. Don't create clutter.

---

case study Jim's boss gave him a new project. At first Jim thought it was relatively straightforward but, after a second meeting with his boss, realized it was not as simple as he first thought. He decided to write a pattern diagram of all the main aspects of the project, and then began to set up a schedule, planning the various stages and listing the work he

---

■ **Work out when you're at your best.** Know what time of day you work to your best ability, and try to protect that time for completing tasks that require the most thought.

■ **Develop an effective work pattern.** Work in concentrated periods, and make sure you take regular breaks. Deal with the urgent and important tasks as much as possible.

■ **Use your slack time.** Have tasks to work on at odd moments.

■ **Delegate where you can.** Give clear instructions when you do so.

■ **Be clear about your role.** Clarify your role with your boss and find out the expectations he or she has of you.

■ **Communicate effectively.** Make better use of meetings and use email and phone calls in a controlled way.

■ **Learn to say no.** Say "no" to stop yourself being overwhelmed.

■ **Eleviate stress.** Develop ways that work for you to reduce stress. Control the way you work to free up time for exercise and relaxation.

Managing your time well ultimately means managing your life well.

could delegate to colleagues in other departments or outsource. He sketched in dates of meetings with various colleagues involved at key stages of the project. It was a full morning's work, but he had achieved a lot. He was confident he could present the outline to his boss and, after some discussion, they agreed the presentation.

Jargon buster

Coach
To guide a person to develop in his or her work, relationships, and role in an organization.

Delegate
To give duties, responsibilities or authority to someone so that he or she can act on your behalf.

Executive summary
An overall summary of a whole report.

Facilitator
A person who helps another person or organization to achieve a particular purpose.

Gantt chart
A chart that illustrates the duration of certain tasks alongside regular periods of time (weeks, months etc); it is useful for planning and scheduling.

Hacker
A person who breaks into the computer system of a person, company or some other organization.

Macro
A group of computer commands that you set up to be automatically performed by a single click.

Mentor
To coach a person, especially with longer-term life issues.

Outsourcing
The passing of work to an outside company. It could be a whole project or part thereof.

Paraphrase
To express something using different words.

Pattern diagram
A creative diagram drawn to generate and capture ideas around a central key word.

Prioritize
To single out and deal with aspects of work or a particular project that are deemed the most important parts.

Proactive
Taking the initiative and deciding what you want to do – in contrast to being reactive, which is acting in response to external pressures and what has already happened.

Reactive
see Proactive.

Spam
Unwanted email sent to a large number of people at the same time.

Standard paragraphs
Text in paragraphs that is used across a range of documents as a basis for individual emails, letters, reports etc.

Strategy
The long-term plans that will fulfil your major aims.

Synergy
The combined effect of people working successfully together that is greater than the sum of each individual's work.

Synonym
A word that has the same, or a similar, meaning as another, e.g. big and large.

Tactics
The plans that are taken to implement a strategy.

Thesaurus
A dictionary of synonyms, arranged either by theme (in the style of Roget's Thesaurus: see the Further reading section) or alphabetically.

'To do' list
A list of all the tasks that a person needs to complete on a particular day.

Further reading

Publications

Augsburger, David *Caring Enough to Hear and to Be Hear*d (Regal Books, 1982) ISBN 978 083 0708369

Buzan, Tony *Mind Mapping* (BBC, 2006) ISBN 978 0563 520344

Covey, Stephen R. *7 Habits of Highly Effective People* (Simon & Schuster, 2004) ISBN 978 068 4858395

Davidson, George *Roget's Thesaurus of English Words and Phrases* (Penguin Books, 2004) ISBN 978 0140515039

Leigh, Judith *Organizing and Participating in Meetings* (Oxford University Press, 2002) ISBN 978 019866 2846

Mackenzie, Alec *The Time Trap: The Classic Book on Time Management* (Amacom, 3rd edition, 1997) ISBN 978 0814479261

Manser, Martin H. (Editor) *Chambers Thesaurus* (Chambers, 3rd edition, 2009) ISBN 978 0550 103338

Manser, Martin H. and Curtis, Stephen *Penguin Writer's Manual* (Penguin, 2003) ISBN 978 0140 514 896

Maxwell, John C. *Developing the Leader Within You* (Thomas Nelson, 2006) ISBN 978 0785 281122

Trask, R.L. *How to Write Effective Emails* (Penguin, 2005) ISBN 978 0141 017198

Websites

www.lcc.arts.ac.uk/courses/36832.htm For courses led by Martin Manser on Time Management, Organizing Effective Meetings and Leadership (University of the Arts London: London College of Communication).

www.lcc.arts.ac.uk/courses/36844.htm Courses by Martin Manser on Confident Written Communications, Business Writing (University of the Arts London: London College of Communication).

www.martinmanser.com/ M/MMTraining.aspx For courses by Martin Manser on Report Writing and English Grammar.

www.capita-LD.co.uk
For courses on which Martin Manser is an
associate trainer, leading courses on writing
(Capita Learning and Development).

www.mindjet.com
A website with visual mind-mapping
software that enables users to interact
visually with information.

www.opp.co.uk
A website giving details of assessment tools
to help you discover your personality type.

www.getorganizednow.com
Tips and ideas on becoming more
organized at work and home.

www.mindtools.com
Guidance on developing your skills
in business.

www.BusinessSecrets.net